# *Design and Make*
# TOYS THAT MOVE

## Helen Greathead

# FRANKLIN WATTS
LONDON • SYDNEY

# Contents

# Introduction

Moving toys have been around for much longer than you might think! The spinning top must be one of the oldest toys. It's also one of the simplest to make.

## Changing technology

All through history, as new technology has changed our way of life, toys have changed, too. Toy trains became popular soon after real trains were invented in the 1800s. The first pull-along wooden trains came out in the 1840s. By the 1870s, tin-plate trains were powered by clockwork mechanisms or steam. By the end of the century, German toy companies were making train tracks, and other accessories.

## Building bricks

Frank Hornby started his toy-making business in 1901 after making a collection of metal bricks that connected together with nuts and bolts. The idea was to encourage his son's interest in engineering. The bricks caught on, and soon, more complex construction kits were on sale. Children could build a skyscraper, or even a ship, or aeroplane! The kits are still highly popular with children today.

## Fantastic plastic

The Second World War stopped toy production in Britain, as factories were needed to make weapons instead. In the USA some toy factories stayed open, but toys were never quite the same! After the war, wood and tin plate were out, and plastic was in! Plastic was easy to mould, quick to produce and cheap to buy.

## Transforming toys

Toys then became more complex and exciting in the way they were made. The 1980s featured popular toys such as Transformers, which changed from things like planes and cars into robots. These toys were simply a matter of clever mechanisms. Meanwhile, Japanese toy makers developed new ideas for toys that were battery operated. Batteries had been used before to make sounds and flashing lights, but the new toys could now move, too.

## Making toys

In this book you can find out how to design and make your own moving toys. From the simple spinning top, to a battery-operated alien, you can try your hand at making all kinds of mechanisms. But whichever toy projects you choose, make sure you have fun designing and making them, as well as playing with them!

# Be prepared

Here is a list of all the materials and equipment you will need to make the different toys in this book.

## Hints and tips
* Always read the instructions all the way through BEFORE you start.
* Clear plenty of space to work in.
* Always try laying things out before you put your model together.
* Take time to think about your ideas. If you get stuck, talk your problem through with a friend or an adult.

## Things to collect

Bodkin

Needles and thread

Compass

Hole punch

Craft knife

Pencils and pens

Hacksaw

Dowel – wooden and basla wood – various lengths and widths

Straws

Lollypop sticks

Boxes of all shapes and sizes

Ready-made wheels

Old-fashioned pegs

Rikrak

Pipe-cleaners

Polystyrene balls

Embroidery thread

Plastic pots/cartons

Buttons

String

Self-hardening clay or Plasticine

Stick-on eyes

Felt-tip pens

Pompoms

Shiny scraps of paper and fabric

Paints

Glow-in-the-dark paint

Netting – from bags of oranges, lemons or chocolate coins

Beads

Feathers

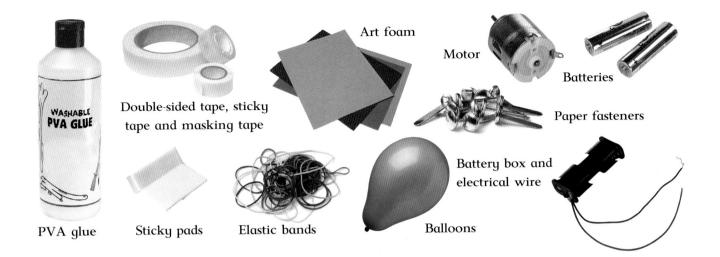

Art foam

Motor

Batteries

Double-sided tape, sticky tape and masking tape

Paper fasteners

Battery box and electrical wire

PVA glue

Sticky pads

Elastic bands

Balloons

# Wheels

✳ You can use all sorts of things for wheels. Collect up old plastic lids, cartons, cardboard tubes of different shapes and sizes and try them out.

✳ Ready-made wheels probably work best, though (see page 31 for stockists).

✳ Dowel makes an ideal axle. Balsa dowel can be cut with a craft knife, but be careful, it breaks easily.

✳ Measure carefully to work out where the holes for the axles should be. They will need to align on each side.

✳ Once the body of your vehicle is finished, attach the wheels to the dowel using strong adhesive. You might need to taper the dowel to fit. (Try using a pencil sharpener for wooden dowel.)

✳ Don't make the wheels fit too closely to the sides of your vehicle. Put a small disc in-between the wheel and the vehicle to help the wheels turn.

✳ String also makes a good axle, as long as you tie it very tightly.

MAKING HOLES

✳ Make a very small hole to start with, and gradually make it bigger.

✳ Always check whether the hole you make needs to hold something firmly or to allow for some movement.

# Spiral spinning top

Here's a really simple moving
toy that's easy to make, too.

## Design and select

Make a simple spinning top with a spiral pattern.
Choose your materials and sketch some ideas before
you start. We used thin card, a short pencil, a compass
and paint. You could use glow-in-the-dark paint
to make the top extra special!

## Make

**1** Use a compass to draw
a circle on a piece of brightly
coloured card. Make a mark in
the middle with the compass point.
Carefully cut out the circle.

**2** Decorate the circle with
an interesting design using
paint. Start at the centre where
you made your mark and
work outwards. Leave
it somewhere safe to dry.

### Challenge
Try using different materials to make a
top. What other shapes can you use?

**3** Use a short pencil to make the shaft of the top.

## Challenge
What else could you use for the shaft?

**4** Carefully make a hole in the middle of the circle with the point of the pencil and push it through. The card should just fit on the pencil. Don't push it up too high!

## Challenge
Experiment to find the best position of the circle on the shaft. When does it spin the longest?

**5** Find a large, flat and smooth surface. Turn out the lights and spin the top on the point of the pencil.

# Pop-up surprise

This pop-up surprise is simple to make but very effective.

## Design and select

Make a colourful pop-up surprise. Look at pictures of animals or people and sketch some ideas. We've made a Chinese dragon. What materials will you use? We used card, a cork, green lamé fabric, pompoms and dowel.

## Look at this!

Here's a fabulous Chinese dragon to give you some inspiration! This one is used at Chinese New Year.

✳ How do you think this dragon moves?

## Make

**1** Draw a semi-circle on a piece of card and cut it out. Cut a piece of your fabric 2–3 cm larger than the card and glue onto one side, sticking down the edges neatly on the other side. Bend the card to make a cone and glue together. Bend it round the dowel rod to get it the right size, but don't stick it to the rod.

**2** Cut a long strip of the fabric the same length as the dowel rod. Sew it into a tube, right-sides together, leaving about 4 cm unstitched at one end. Turn the tube the right way out.

**3** Push the dowel through the tube with the unstitched end at the bottom. Gather the top end of the tube and stick to the dowel with sticky tape.

**4** At the other end of the fabric tube, cut some slits in the material. Push the cone you made earlier onto the end of the dowel rod and stick the material down inside the cone. Decorate the cone with rikrak.

**5** Cut out a head and nose from shiny card. Stick half a cork on the face so that the nose juts out. Add a tongue, some fur and horns. Stick on small pompoms for eyes.

## Challenge
How else could you make the head more 3-D?

**6** Use sticky pads and double-sided tape to attach the head to the dowel rod and bend a piece of card for the back of the head (right). Make your creature pop up!

# *Hopalong hen*

This hen almost looks real as it bobs up and down!

## Design and select

Make a pushalong bobbing bird for a toddler. Draw some bird sketches and think about which ones will work best. How can you decorate them? We used strong card, paint, art foam, feathers, stick-on eyes and a balsa dowel rod.

## Look at this!

This wooden toy duck clatters along as you push it.

✱ Why doesn't it have round wheels?

✱ Which part of the duck moves as it rolls along?

## Make

1 Draw your bird on a piece of card, cut out two shapes and decorate one side of each piece. Make sure they are the opposite sides.

### Challenge
What else could you use to make the body?

2 Make wheels from thick cardboard. Pierce a hole off-centre with the tip of a pencil in the same place on both wheels. Paint them a bright colour.

12

**3** Get an adult to help you make a hole through the balsa dowel, 1 cm from the end (you can use a bodkin). Make a hole with a hole punch 1 cm from the bottom of each hen, making sure they are in exactly the same position on each hen.

## Challenge
Could you make a bird with wings that flap?

**4** Thread some thick string through the balsa dowel and then through the hole in the hens, placing one on each side of the dowel. Add a wheel on each side and tie a knot in the string to hold them on securely.

**5** Attach the hen pieces to the dowel with sticky pads and stick the hen together at the head and tail with more sticky pads. Stick on some feathers to make a tail. Push your hen along and watch it bob!

## Challenge
Make your bird rattle as it rolls!

# Sparkly mobile

## Blow on this mobile and watch it move!

## Look at this!

Alexander Calder made sculptures out of wire. He made some enormous mobiles! His sculptures are described as kinetic art, because they move.

✱ What materials do you think Calder used to make the fish?

✱ How did he attach the shapes?

## Design and select

Design a fish mobile and decorate it with sparkly shapes. Sketch some designs for your fish shapes. How will the pieces of your mobile connect? We used pipe cleaners, wool, net (from a bag of oranges), stick-on eyes, felt and anything shiny!

## Make

1 Bend and twist a pipe cleaner to make a fish shape. Make four shapes in all.

twist right round here →

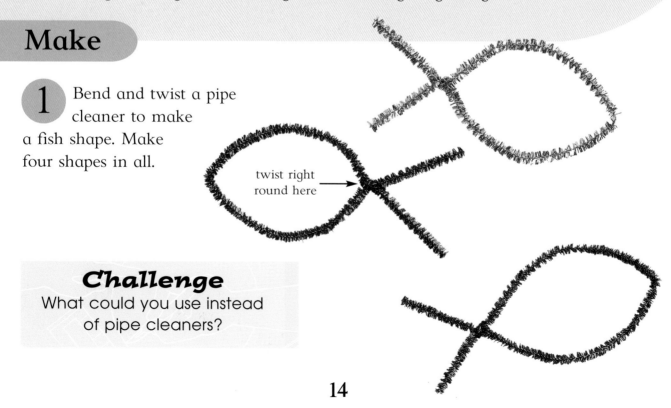

### Challenge
What could you use instead of pipe cleaners?

**2** Cut a piece of net a bit bigger than your fish. Use a needle and thread to sew the netting onto the pipe cleaner. Wind the thread through the holes in the net to hold it on.

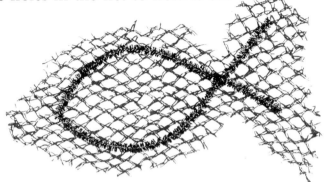

**3** Glue on eyes made out of a circle of felt and a plastic eye. Tie or glue sequins and beads to the net and stick on bits of shiny fabric and paper.

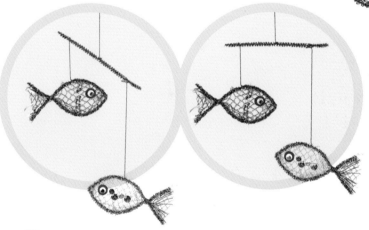

**4** Cut pipe cleaners in half to use as rods, and tie on the fish loosely, with wool. Connect the mobile together as we have (right). Hang up the mobile and push the wool along the rods to make it balance. The rods need to be horizontal.

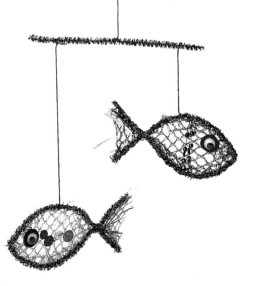

## Challenge
How could you add more fish to the mobile?

# Lift-up ladder engine

Make a fire engine
that really works.

## Design and select

Make a fire engine with a lift-up ladder
and a wind-up hose. Choose your materials.
We used a washing tablet box, ready-made
wheels, dowel, wooden lolly sticks, paints, an
elastic band, a paper fastener, a pipe cleaner,
string and a long balloon.

## Make

**1** Cut the top off your box and give it a coating
of red paint — the open side of the box will
be the bottom of your engine. Make four holes for
the wheels using your ready-made wheels and
a ruler to work out how high up these
should be. The guidelines (right) show
where to place your wheels.

**2** To make the ladder rungs, get an adult to help
you cut lolly sticks in half with scissors. Glue the
rungs onto four uncut sticks to make the ladder — it needs
to be the same length as your box. Paint the ladder silver.

16

**3** Use a craft knife to make two holes for the ladder in the roof (left). The front hole needs to be long and as wide as the square dowel (see step 5).

**4** Tie an elastic band around the second rung of the ladder. Push the band through the smaller hole. Wrap the other end of the elastic band around a small piece of dowel to hold it loosely in place (right).

**5** To lift the ladder, you need a lever. Ask an adult to help you make this by cutting two pieces of square dowel. One should be 4 cm wider than the box, the other should be two thirds of the height of the box. Tape the pieces together to form a T-shape with the longer piece forming the top of the T. Paint the T silver.

**6** Ask for help to make a slit in each side of the box so that the lever can move up and down. Add a notch at the top to hold the lever in place, as shown below. Work out the curve of the slit with a compass, starting one third up the box, as shown right.

**7** Push the lever inside the box and poke the ends out of the slits on each side. Tape the central bar of the lever onto the ladder through the large hole in the top of the box. Move the lever to work the ladder.

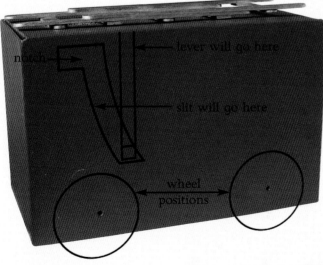

notch

lever will go here

slit will go here

wheel positions

### Challenge
How could you add a roll-up door?

**17**

continued ➞

**8** To make the wind-up hose, cut two discs of card 5 cm in diameter and paint them black. Attach one to the end of your engine with a paper fastener – get an adult to help you. Cut a 2 cm strip from a narrow cardboard tube and glue it to the centre of the other card disc. Make a hole in the disc inside the cardboard tube.

Disc

Cardboard tube

**9** Cut a piece of pipe cleaner about 6 cm long and push through the hole you just made. Tape the end down securely on the inside of the cardboard tube. Fold over the other end of the pipe cleaner to make a handle. Glue the tube onto the disc you fastened to the engine. The cross-section picture, right, shows you how all the sections connect. Now stick on a long balloon to make the hose.

## Challenge
Make a light for the roof!

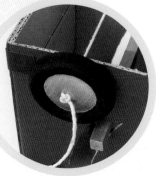

**10** Paint your ready-made wheels. Use strong string for the axles, thread it through the holes you made in step 1, and tie on the wheels.

**11** Add more decoration to your engine, like windows and doors. Now it's ready to roll!

## Challenge
Use some of these techniques to make a digger that lifts up its loader.

# Shark shock

This toy uses a cam mechanism to make it bob up and down.

## Design and select

Use a cam mechanism to make a shark shoot out of the sea! Think about the look of your shark, look at some references and sketch your ideas. What materials will you use? We used strong card, wooden dowel, art foam, sticky pads and stick-on eyes.

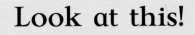

## Look at this!

Turn the handle on this machine, and the boat sinks, then rises again.

✱ What is it made from?

✱ How do you think the cat moves?

## Make

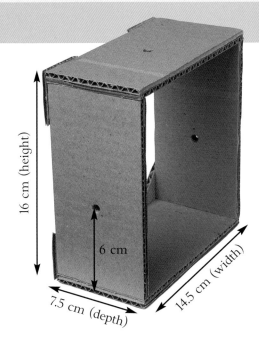

16 cm (height)

6 cm

7.5 cm (depth)

14.5 cm (width)

1  Make a box from strong cardboard like this, 14.5 cm (width) by 16 cm (height) and 7.5 cm (depth). Add triangular supports at each corner on the back, shown right. Pierce a small hole with a pencil in the centre of the top and one in each side, 6 cm up from the bottom.

2  Get help to cut a piece of dowel with a hacksaw, 20 cm long. Cut out a disc of card with a 6 cm diameter and make a hole in it off centre. Now, push the dowel through one of the holes on the side, through the hole in the disc and then through the hole in the other side of the box. Wind some tape around each end of the dowel to hold it in place.

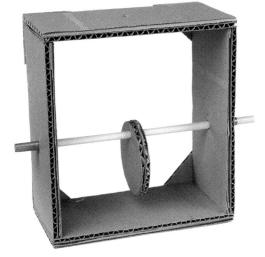

**3** Cut out another disc of card 6 cm in diameter and make a hole in its centre. Cut a piece of dowel the same height as the box. Push this through the hole in the top of the box and glue the disc on its bottom.

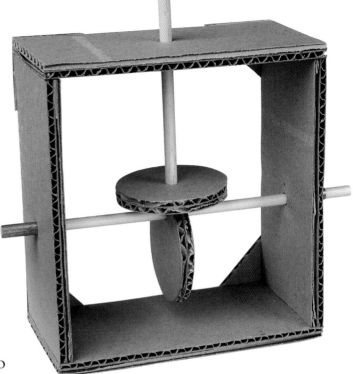

**4** To make a handle for your machine, cut out a rectangle of card 2 cm by 4 cm and make two holes in it. Cut a piece of dowel 3 cm long and push through one hole of the rectangle. Push the other end onto the horizontal dowel, as shown below.

**5** To make the shark, fold a piece of art foam in half, draw on half a shark shape and cut it out carefully.

**6** Use sticky pads to stick the sides of the shark together at the front and back. Don't fold the tail over but make a slit in it so that it will stick up. Make slits for the gills and add stick-on eyes. Glue the shark in position on the vertical dowel.

**Challenge**
Add another cam to make a swimmer bob up and down in the water!

**7** Cut and decorate some paper to look like the sea and stick it on the front. Turn the handle and watch out for the shark!

# Balloon racing car

Blow up the balloon and watch this car go, go, go!

## Look at this!

This car is made out of plastic and can run fast.

**✷** Why do you think the balloon makes the car move?

**✷** Why do you think the car is made of plastic?

## Design and select

Make a racing car that is powered by an ordinary balloon! Choose your materials, sketch out your ideas. Remember that this car needs to be really light. We made the car using art foam, straws, a balloon, cardboard and sticky pads.

## Make

1 Cut out a rectangle of foam, lightly score a line lengthways down the middle with a craft knife. Fold in half. Draw on the shape of half your racing car with the top of the car on the fold and cut it out carefully. Make holes in the sides for the axles. Stick the foam together at the front with a sticky pad.

**2** Make the wheels out of four circles of cardboard, make two of them a bit smaller for the front wheels. Cut them out and paint them black and silver.

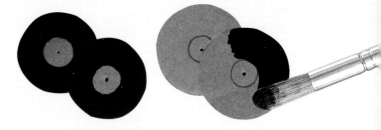

**3** Cut pieces of straw for the axles and slot them through the holes in the sides of the car. Add a dab of glue onto the ends of the straw and stick on the wheels.

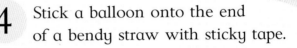

**4** Stick a balloon onto the end of a bendy straw with sticky tape.

### Challenge
Try putting the balloon in different positions to see if it still works.

**5** Slot the straw underneath the foam body of the car above the axles with the balloon at the front. Secure the end with tape.

**6** Blow through the straw to inflate the balloon. Quickly put the car on a smooth surface and watch it whizz away! (If your car stops working, try changing the balloon.)

### Challenge
Can you decorate the car, without making it too heavy?

# *Roll-along monster*

This monster's mood
changes as it rolls along!

## Design and select

Design a moving monster powered by an elastic band!
Sketch different facial expressions first, then choose your
materials. We used card, a strong elastic band, two
straws and some wooden dowel.

## Make

**1** To make a reel, cut a length
of cardboard tube slightly wider
than your elastic band. Cut two card
discs for the ends with a diameter
about twice the size of the tube. Use
a pencil to make holes in their centre
big enough for a straw to go through.

**2** Stick the discs to
the tube with either
glue or tape.

**3** Cut a piece from a thick straw, just longer
than the reel. Push it through the hole in one
disc and out of the hole on the other side of the reel.
Make the straw stick out more on one side.

**4** Make a hook from a paper clip and use it to thread the elastic band through the straw. Use a small piece of dowel to hold the band on one side of the reel. Pull the band tight and tape down the dowel.

**5** Push a full-length straw through the top of the elastic band so that it rests on the straw through the centre of the reel.

**6** Measure a strip of paper to wrap around the tube. Create two different faces on the strip one above the other — one happy, one angry. Stick to the reel.

## Challenge
How could you make a hat for the monster? Where would you have to attach it?

**7** Wind the long straw round and round until you can feel the elastic band tightening. Put the monster on a smooth surface and watch it roll towards you!

## Challenge
Try making moving monsters from lots of different containers.

# *Rapunzel's wind-up prince*

Rapunzel lived in a tall tower and a
prince climbed up her plait to visit her.
Make life easier for Rapunzel and
pull the prince up for her!

## Design and select

Make a tower with a pulley to lift Rapunzel's
hair. Sketch some pictures to see how the pulley
will work. We used a cereal box, balsa dowel,
waxed linen thread, a plastic tub, old-fashioned
wooden pegs, felt, paint, embroidery thread,
pipe cleaners, felt-tip pens and stick-on eyes.

## Make

1   Cut off a section of a cereal box, about two
    thirds of its width will do. Make a slit in the
side near the top and push in half a plastic tub to
make the balcony. Stick the tub down at the sides.
Give the tower and balcony a coating of paint.

2   Cut off a corner from the left-over
    cereal box and paint the same colour
as the tower. Make holes through its sides
and push a piece of dowel about 10 cm
long through the holes. This is your pulley.
Stick one end of a piece of waxed thread
50 cm long to the centre of the dowel. Stick
the pulley on top of the tower with the open
part facing the front (see page 27).

26

**3** Make peg dolls for Rapunzel and the prince. Glue pipe cleaners onto the pegs for arms and make simple outfits out of felt. Draw on faces with felt-tip pens and stick on plastic eyes. Plait some embroidery thread to make Rapunzel's hair. It should be a little longer than the cereal box. Stick it firmly onto her head.

## Challenge
How could you make the witch in the story pop up in the tower?

**4** Stick Rapunzel in the tower and weave the loose end of the waxed thread through her plait. Wrap the prince's arms around the plait (right) and tie on securely with some thread.

## Challenge
How could you pull the prince up using a motor?

**5** Make a turret roof from a semi-circle of card (see page 10) and stick on top of the tower. Paint on bricks and windows. Turn the pulley to pull up the prince!

# Battery-operated alien

Press a switch to make
the alien dizzy!

## Design and select

Make a toy alien using a battery-operated circuit to spin
its head round. Think about your design and sketch some
ideas. Choose your materials. We've used a polystyrene
ball, a yoghurt pot and some Plasticine. You will need
some batteries, a battery box, some electrical wire, paper
fasteners, card, paint and a small motor.

## Make

**1** Cut out a large circle of card for the circuit base.

**2** Your battery box will probably have two
wires attached to it. Ask for help to
strip off the plastic on the ends of the
wires. Attach one of the wires to the
motor, twisting it around the hooks as shown, right.
Attach another wire to the other side of the motor.

**3** Cut a small hole in the bottom of the yoghurt
pot. Push the top of the motor through the hole
and secure it inside the yoghurt pot with Plasticine.

**4** Make a switch from a folded square of card with a paper fastener pushed through each side. Make sure the heads of the paper fasteners are on the inside of the switch and that they touch when you fold it closed.

**5** Wind the free wire from the motor around the back of the paper fastener, as shown, left. Do the same with the free wire from the battery box to complete the circuit. Tape the circuit to the cardboard base.

**6** Press the switch to ensure that the circuit works. If it doesn't, check that the wires are connected properly.

**7** Decorate a polystyrene ball to make the alien's head and push it on top of the motor. Decorate the pot to make the alien's body. Cover the circuit with paper and paint to make it look like a space landscape. Press the switch and watch your alien spin!

### Challenge
Could you make the whole robot spin round?

# Glossary

**adhesive**
something that makes things stick

**aligned**
to put things into a straight line
or in line with each other

**axle**
a bar or rod on which a wheel
or set of wheels turns

**balsa wood**
lightweight wood used to make
model boats and aeroplanes

**bodkin**
a blunt, thick needle to thread
elastic or tape

**cam**
a projecting part on a rotating wheel
which makes another part move

**dowel**
thin, wooden rod

**kinetic**
to do with or produced by
movement

**lamé**
material that has a shiny coating

**lever**
a handle used to operate or control
a piece of machinery

**mechanism**
the moving parts of a machine

**notch**
a small cut in a surface or on
the edge of something

**pulley**
a wheel with a grooved rim in which
a pulled rope or chain can run

**right-sides**
the side of the material that you
want to show

**taper**
to become gradually narrower
or thinner towards one end

# *Further information*

You might find these websites helpful for finding
ideas, techniques and materials:

**www.historychannel.com/
exhibits/toys/chess.html** – for a
timeline of toys through the ages.

**www.nga.gov/exhibitions/calder/
realsp/room11-10.htm** – for a virtual
tour of an exhibition of Alexander
Calder's work.

**www.enchantedlearning.com/
crafts/mobiles** – more ideas for
mobiles you can make.

**www.howstuffworks.com** – to find
out more about the mechanisms
used in this book.

**www.balloonhq.com/balloon_
car/balloon_car.html** – check out
this site for some brilliant model
balloon cars including pictures and
descriptions of how they were made.

**http://storypalace.ourfamily.com/
c98B23.html** – this site includes the
story of Rapunzel.

**www.technologystudent.com/cams
/cam2.htm** – to see an example of a
working cam.

**http://automata.co.uk/gallery.htm**
– go to this site for some more ideas
for how to use the cam mechanism.

**www.walterruffler.de/
Designs.html** – this site shows 25 cam
models made out of paper.

**www.nyu.edu/pages/
linguistics/courses/v610051/
gelmanr/** – take a look through this
gallery of historical automata.

**www.mos.org/sln/Leonardo/
LeosMysteriousMachinery.html** -
take a look at some of the amazing
machines invented by Leonardo Da
Vinci ... then try to work out what
they were used for!

**www.childrensscrapstore.co.uk** –
information about the Children's
scrapstore in Bristol, where scrap
materials are recycled and sold for
educational art and craft projects.

**www.modelshop.co.uk** – for all kinds
of craft supplies, including ready-
made wheels, balsa dowel, pulley
wheels, motors etc.

Every effort has been made by the Publisher to ensure that
these websites are suitable for children, and contain no inappropriate
or offensive material. However, because of the nature of the
Internet, it is impossible to guarantee that the contents
of these sites will not be altered. We strongly advise that Internet
access is supervised by a responsible adult.

# Index

First published in 2005 by
Franklin Watts, 96 Leonard Street
London EC2A 4XD

Franklin Watts Australia
Level 17/207 Kent Street, Sydney, NSW 2000

© Franklin Watts 2005

**Editor:** Rachel Tonkin; **Art Director:** Jonathan Hair;
**Design:** Matthew Lilly and Anna-Marie D'Cruz; **Photography:** Steve Shott.
**Picture credits:** Comstock Images/Alamy: 4c. © Dig. Image MoMA,
New York/Scala. © 2005 DACS London & ARS New York: 14t. Stock
Connection Distribution/Alamy: 10t. Every attempt has been made
to clear copyright. Should there be any inadvertent omission please
apply to the Publisher for rectification.

The Publisher wishes to thank Keith Newstead for
permission to use the picture on page 19.
The author wishes to thank Patricia Greathead,
Laurie Greathead, Angus McCubbine and Sacha Baker.

A CIP catalogue record for this book
is available from the British Library

Dewey Classification: 688.7'28
ISBN 0 7496 6070 8
Printed in China